A Hap[...]tices
to Survive Your Teenage Years

By: Daniel R. Mitchell PhD
Illustration by Fred Sovie

Acknowledgements

I would like to express my gratitude to the many patients and their family members, colleagues and mentors for all that you have taught me. Thanks to my niece, Felicia Mitchell who is pictured on the cover of the book. I thank Fred for his patience and great sense of humor. I thank the many loved ones who gave me excellent feedback on the many drafts of this book. I thank my wonderfully supportive family, especially my wife and parents. To my dearest daughter Mallory, I hope someday you might find the skills in this book useful in surviving YOUR teenage years. The day I married your mom and the day you were born were the greatest moments of my life.

"Nothing that is worthwhile is ever easy." – Indira Ghandi

Introduction – How to use this book

Dear Reader: Thank you for taking this step towards a happier teenage existence. This book is intended to be used much like a recipe book. In fact, you could open this book to a random page if you like. The most important key to this book is DOING, not just reading. In fact, I recommend that you do not try to read this book from start to finish. How about that!? A book you don't have to read all the way through! As you find strategies you really like, use a post it note, bookmark, or fold the page corner to mark your spot. Feel free to use the extra space in each page to write notes to yourself. This is a book you use by following the strategy you are reading in the moment. In fact, the whole book encourages being in the moment instead of fretting over the past or worrying about the future.

Please note a few cautions. While I encourage you to try each strategy, I caution you to never do anything that would cause an unsafe situation. I also encourage you to be sure that when doing these activities, you are not getting yourself in trouble, disrupting others (such as a classroom), or making anyone else feel bad or unsafe. Most importantly, if you are feeling depressed or extremely anxious, I would urge you to tell an adult you trust, like a parent or guidance counselor, or see your doctor. This book is meant to be therapeutic, not therapy.

Again, thank you for reading. Be well and be happy!

Grateful

Make a list of "gratefuls". It is so important to remember the things you like about your life. Make a list either on paper or in your cell phone (perhaps as a text) and carry it with you wherever you go. When life gets you down, read your list to remind you of the good stuff.

Tip: Don't make your gratefuls conditional (e.g., "I like my mom when she is being nice").

Sleep

Sleep is really important, but it is just as important to make your sleep a rhythm. Tonight, when you are getting ready for bed, follow these steps.

1. Try your very best to NOT take a nap during the daytime.
2. Choose a decent bedtime that will give you a good amount of rest.
3. About 30 to 60 minutes before bedtime, put away your electronics and do something calming. Taking a bath or reading a good book are possibilities for this task.
4. Next, prepare your room for sleep by making it dark, preparing your bed so it is as comfortable as possible, and putting away homework.
5. Last but not least, if you have any issues that are bothering you or making you worry, make a note of those issues on a piece of paper, and putting it somewhere you will find it in the morning.
6. Go to bed.

Tip: If you have an urge to nap, do something while standing up or an activity that requires a lot of movement until you aren't tired anymore or it is time for bed.

Unplug!

At least once a day, turn off your phone, your TV, your computer and any other electronic devices you have for a little while.

Tip: A great time to unplug is right before bedtime.

Rant-Free

If you are involved in social media websites like Facebook® or Myspace®, only add friends or keep friends that are positive when they interact with you. This does not mean you have to block friends who post "rants" on their timeline or wall, because remember, they are not directing it at you unless they use your name.

Tip: Don't post rants. It will cause others to get upset with you, which in turn will cause even more stress. Instead, if you want to use social media to communicate your frustrations pick a few close friends and message them. That way you are more likely to get the support you are seeking.

Belly Laugh

Laugh at least once a day. If you are having a hard time finding something to laugh about, do something silly. Remember, if those around you are grumpy, sad, or serious then you will be more likely to be grumpy. If you are cheery, positive and silly, those around you will be more likely to do the same.

Get Organized

Spend just a few minutes (maybe 5-10 minutes) in the morning, afternoon, and evening to get organized.

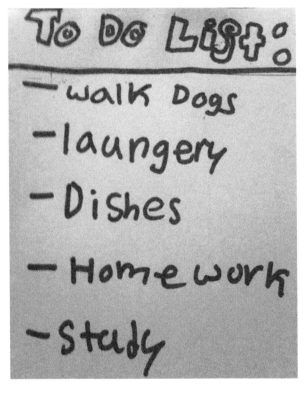

*Photography by Elizabeth C. Hahn

Funny Face

Make the strangest, weirdest face you possibly can and snap a picture (maybe with a digital camera or a cell phone) and send it to a family member or close friend. See what happens.

Pet a pet!

Petting an animal can feel very calming, especially furry ones! Dogs and cats seem to have the ability to de-stress their human companions. So today, give your pet a few nice gentle strokes with your hand.

Tip: If you don't have one, go find the pet of someone you know. Just make sure to ask permission from the owner and be sure the pet is friendly!

*Photography by Elizabeth C. Hahn

Pay a Compliment

Give someone you care about a compliment. It doesn't matter what it is as long as you feel it is true.

Tip: When paying a compliment to someone, remember that some people have a hard time accepting compliments, so don't be upset if you don't get the response you were expecting. Don't argue with them if they disagree, just say "agree to disagree".

Be a Helper

Volunteer to help someone out and go out of your way to not get anything in return.

Tip: This can be something really simple, like offering to hold a door open, or really complex, like volunteering at the local animal shelter.

Get Your Motor Running

Eat breakfast every morning. Eating something healthy in the morning will help your mood and your ability to concentrate, so you may be less likely to get frustrated in class.

Tip: A piece of toast with peanut butter is easy and cheap to make and can fill you up to get you through until lunch.

Binder Organizer

Make a binder for school that has a front and back pocket. Label your pockets so that your unfinished assignments go in the front and your finished assignments to be turned in go in the back.

Tip: Make sure you check your binder often. It is so frustrating to not get credit for something you completed! Try and get in the habit of checking your binder at the beginning and end of each class.

Getting Your Morning Right

Keep all things you need to get ready in the morning (glasses, deodorant, and medications) in the same location (like a spot in your bathroom or your bedside table) instead of having them in several different places.

Laugh Off

Find a good playful joke (no dirty ones please) and tell it over and over to as many people as possible. Laughing is ok as long as it is not at someone's expense. It is also OK to laugh at yourself as long as it is not at your expense.

Tip: It is a bad habit to rely only on electronics (such as social media) to laugh.

Happy Music

We often tend to gravitate towards music that magnifies our mood. What this means is, if you are angry, you listen to angry music like heavy metal or gangster rap. The same holds true for when we are happy. Make a play list of songs you listen to when you are having a really good day. Make it your "happy list". When you are feeling down or angry or some other negative emotion, play your happy list instead of the things you normally listen to when you are upset.

Tip: You can use an Ipod, your IPhone or Smart Phone, music software, or even make a mixed CD.

The Good List

Make a list of all the things you like about yourself or that others like about you. Store it somewhere. You can even do this on an electronic device. Save it, and each time you think of something new, add it to your list. When you are having a bad day, look at your list and read it aloud. Reading it aloud is a VERY important step, so don't skip it unless you are somewhere that is not appropriate (like in a classroom).

Sing Out Loud!

Sing something you know the words to or download the lyrics and sing the song all the way through. Just make SURE it is a song that makes you HAPPY. See "Happy Music" on page 19 for help on this.

Getting Busy

Start a new hobby or interest. Starting this process may be easy, like grabbing paper and a pencil from your desk and start drawing, or multi-steps like calling around to find prices for martial arts. A lot of hobbies take some work to get all "your ducks in a row" but if you go step by step, you will eventually get to try something you are interested in.

Tip: There are a lot of great hobbies that don't cost a thing. Try asking your guidance counselor at school for a list of clubs as a place to start.

*Photography by Elizabeth C. Hahn

Do the Dance

It doesn't matter what music you are dancing to. In fact, you don't even need music but it helps. You could line dance, do a certain routine, or just free style. The part that is important is that you are moving around.

Tip: If you don't like how you dance (most people don't), then dance with your eyes closed or use a strobe light.

Walk It Off

Take a walk, but no matter where or what kind of weather or circumstance, just notice what is around you without judging. For example, if it is loud, just notice the noise, try to describe it in your head or out loud, as if just to observe. If there is snow, notice how it sounds or feels under your feet. This is called being mindful and taking a "non-judgmental stance".

A-Mazing Idea!

Sometimes drawing can help make you feel better. Draw a maze and then give it to a friend to see if they can beat it. Make it as big or as little as you like.

Tip: You could use blank space in this book to make a maze if you like.

*Photography by Elizabeth C. Hahn

Scavenger Hunt

Create a scavenger hunt for your friends. This is done by giving them clues to find more clues and some sort of prize at the end.

Tip: The prize doesn't have to cost anything.

Greeting Card

Make a home-made greeting card for a close friend. You could draw using pencils or markers. You could even make ink thumbprints and draw characters out of them. You could also use a photocopier if you have access to one and take a funny picture of your face squished against the glass.

Thanks!

Say "thank you" to someone you see every day or often but never say "thank you" to, like a friend, a relative, or a teacher. It can be for anything, but it can also be simple like "Thanks for being who you are."

The Smile Game

Smile at someone today and wait until they return the smile. If not, try someone else until you succeed.

Happy Cookies

Bake cookies (if you are allowed) and then eat some. Make sure to give some away to people you care about.

Pet Whisperer

Pets are very good listeners...even the hyper nutty ones. When you have things you need to say but are afraid a human will judge you or make you feel bad, talk to a pet.

My "New" Room

Re-arrange your room or another room in the house (get permission if needed) and then enjoy as if it is a brand new living space.

Pay It Forward

Do something nice for three people and pass each of them a note that asks them to do something nice for three more people.

Any Change?

Change is constant. This means that the only thing you can expect will happen for sure is change. Think of something that has changed in your life recently and come up with something positive that has come of it. If you need help, you can ask someone to help you.

Tip: Make SURE that if you need help from someone it is a person that you know will do a good job helping you come up with something positive. Don't ask the downer people, as they may just make you feel worse!

Shred It!

Think of one negative thing about your day or your life, and write it down in big letters on a piece of paper. Then, shred it! You can use an office paper shredder, scissors or just use your hands. Try to get the paper into as many tiny little pieces as possible. Then, in a symbolic way, "let go" of it by either throwing it in a trash can or burying it in a garden or yard. The garden idea is great because you can take a negative thing and make it positive by making it food for the plants.

Tip: Do NOT burn it! This goes against the purpose of the activity and is unsafe.

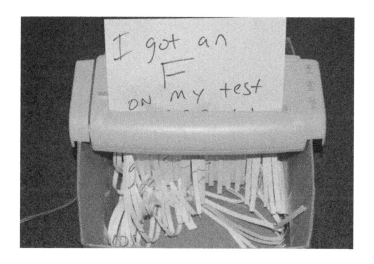

De-Clutter

Throw out or donate three things you no longer need. In doing this, you can de-clutter your life. If it helps, focus on a place in your living space that seems cluttered, especially a place you use often, such as a bed side table or bathroom counter.

Mmmm…Chocolate!

Treat yourself to <u>one</u> piece of chocolate.

Tip: Try mindfully tasting that piece of chocolate. Close your eyes while chewing. Chew slowly and pay close attention to the taste and texture of the chocolate and anything else you might notice.

Go Outside!

If it is sunny out, enjoy being in the sun. Sunlight can be good for you in moderation. If it is raining out, go splash in the puddles. If there are leaves on the ground, gather them and play in the pile. If it is snowy out, go roll around in the snow or make a snow angel.

Tip: Try paying attention to the different sensations (sight, sound, touch, and smell).

*Photography by Elizabeth C. Hahn

Vacation

Take a vacation from your worries. Write yourself a prescription to not worry about anything for a whole day.

The Sculpture Trick

Think about something you might sculpt out of modeling clay. Can you picture it? Now picture yourself sculpting that object BUT you are not allowed to take the clay out of the can! How hard would that be? Think about your thoughts in your head the same way. If you don't take your thoughts out of your head (such as talking or journaling), you may not be able to make sense of them and you will get "stuck". Thoughts cause feelings, and negative thoughts usually cause negative feelings.

Write your thoughts down on a piece of paper when you catch yourself stuck in negative thoughts. Then, "sculpt" the negative thought into something positive. Then repeat it to yourself over and over again.

Singing Off Key

Sing badly on purpose. The badly done melodies just might make you laugh.

Priorities

You can't do it all, so just be ok with that. Instead, write a to-do list and prioritize the top three. Perhaps a few of them can be pages from this book!

Dance Badly

Dance badly on purpose. Make sure you do it in a mirror so you can see just how bad it looks. It might make you laugh, which is the goal.

Tip: You may want to choose an especially silly song for this.

Your Phone as an Organizer

Use your cell phone to set reminders for daily, weekly, or monthly events. For example, if you are supposed to remember to call a relative once a week, this will help you remember, but you have to be ready to do it as soon as your alarm goes off.

Tip: A cell phone is a great way to take pictures, use as an alarm clock, keep a calendar, and use for a calculator; you don't even need to pay cellular or Wi-Fi services, your phone will still work for those other tasks.

Breathe!

Every time you notice you are having a negative thought or feeling, take 3 very deep breaths. Repeat this until you feel better.

Tip: How will you know your thought is negative or is causing a negative reaction? If you are not sure, notice how your body feels. Sometimes our jaw or shoulders tighten, or our face gets hot.

The Yawn Game

Make other people yawn. This can be a fun way to subconsciously get others yawning. Do it in a crowded place if possible and make yourself yawn very deeply. Then look around to see how many people yawn in turn. Yawning is a great way to get a good amount of oxygen in your lungs fast, which can make you feel better.

Tip: Be careful doing this in school. You don't want to disrupt others, such as in the classroom.

New Habit

Try something new (as long as it is HEALTHY), such as a new food, a new route to school or other destination, or some other new experience.

Sharing Your Day

Near the end of your day, sit and talk with someone you care about. First, share a situation that was the worst part of your day. If you did anything to make your day better, be sure to tell them. Then end your discussion with the best part of your day.

Tip: Sharing a meal at the end of the day with your family can be a great time to try this skill. Be sure to limit distractions, such as having the television on.

Jump for Joy

Do 25 jumping jacks and get your heart racing!

I Did It!

Make an "I did it!" list instead of a "To do" list and enjoy knowing the accomplishments you have made.

Tip: Make sure you mention that you started using this book!

Who Nose?

Sniff something that smells good, like a lemon in your fridge or a flower. Your sense of smell is an underused way to feel better.

Stretching

Do a few stretches. Stretching does not require getting on the right clothes or using a yoga mat! You can do this anywhere, even in class while sitting at your desk. Do this several times a day.

Get Inspired!

Read an inspirational book or watch a feel-good movie; something light-hearted, happy or inspirational.

Tip: Some good ideas for movies are: "It's a Wonderful Life", "We Bought a Zoo", or "The Pursuit of Happyness".

Be Genuine, Be You!

I have two very important words for you. <u>Be yourself</u>. I know how hard it is to be a teenager. One of the things we all want more than just about anything is to be accepted. Before you can be accepted by others, you must learn to accept yourself, and just as important, learn that not all your peers will accept you. Why? Because they are teenagers too! Stop trying so hard to be accepted by everyone. In doing this, we tend to get acceptance from no one mainly because we have stopped being ourselves. Do you like fake people? Exactly! Neither do they. If you haven't figured out just who you are yet, relax, most others haven't either, even some adults. Just be genuine. Spend the entire day with absolutely NO sarcasm and make as many genuine statements as you can.